Body Art

PIERCING

Anna Claybourne

Heinemann
LIBRARY

www.heinemann.co.uk/library
Visit our website to find out more information about **Heinemann Library** books.

To order:
☎ Phone 44 (0) 1865 888066
🖹 Send a fax to 44 (0) 1865 314091
💻 Visit the Heinemann Bookshop at www.heinemann.co.uk/library to browse our catalogue and order online.

First published in Great Britain by Heinemann Library, Halley Court, Jordan Hill, Oxford OX2 8EJ, part of Harcourt Education. Heinemann is a registered trademark of Harcourt Education Ltd.

© Harcourt Education Ltd 2004
First published in paperback in 2005
The moral right of the proprietor has been asserted.

Editorial: Lucy Thunder and Helen Cannons
Design: David Poole and Kamae Design
Illustrations: Kamae Design
Picture Research: Rebecca Sodergren and Hannah Taylor
Production: Edward Moore

Originated by Repro Multi-Warna
Printed and bound in China by South China Printing Company
The paper used to print this book comes from sustainable resources.

ISBN 0 431 17924 7 (hardback)
08 07 06 05 04
10 9 8 7 6 5 4 3 2 1

ISBN 0 431 17929 8 (paperback)
09 08 07 06 05
10 9 8 7 6 5 4 3 2 1

British Library Cataloguing in Publication Data

Claybourne, Anna
Piercing. – (Body art)
391.6'5
A full catalogue record for this book is available from the British Library.

Acknowledgements

The Publishers would like to thank the following for permission to reproduce photographs:

Alamy/Bob Jones p**11 bottom**; Alamy/Mark Lewis p**13**; Ancient Art & Architecture Collection/Eric Hobson p**8**; Ancient Art & Architecture Collection/Patrick Syder p**9**; Art Archive/Civiche Racc d'Arte Pavia Italy/Dagli Orti p**22**; Art Archive/Museum of Mankind London/Eileen Tweedy p**17 top**; Corbis/Tiziana & Gianni Baldizzone p**21 top**; Corbis/Jack Fields p**4**; Corbis/Catherine Karnow p**7**; Corbis/Richard Olivier p**20**; Corbis/Bettmann p**18**; The Hutchison Library/Isabella Tree p**25 top**; Imagestate/AGE Fotostock p**14**; Katz Pictures/Benainous-Scorcelletti p**5**; Katz Pictures/Sjodin Graig/ABC-TV/Zuma Press p**27 top**; Magnum Photos/Thomas Hoepker p**23**; Mary Evans Picture Library p**24**; PA Photos/Ian West p**25** bottom; Panos Pictures/J.C. Callow p**11 top**; Panos Pictures/Jean-Leo Dugast p**6**; Panos Pictures/John Miles p**10**; Panos Pictures/Sean Sprague p**26**; PYMCA/David Swindells p**17 bottom**; Rex Features/South West News Service p**27 bottom**; Still Pictures/Adrian Arbib p**15**; Still Pictures/Mark Edwards p**16**; Still Pictures/Michel Gunther p**12**; Topham Picturepoint/PressNet p**29 bottom**; Topham Picturepoint/Universal Pictorial Press Photo p**29 top**; Werner Forman Archive p**19**; Werner Forman Archive/Museum of Northern Arizona p**21 bottom**; Zefa/R. Ross p**28**.

Cover photograph of an Indian girl wearing silver piercings, reproduced with permission of Corbis/Dave Bartruff.

The Publishers would like to thank Jenny Peck, curator at the Pitt Rivers Museum, University of Oxford, for her assistance in the preparation of this book.

Every effort has been made to contact copyright holders of any material reproduced in this book. Any omissions will be rectified in subsequent printings if notice is given to the publishers.

Disclaimer

CONTENTS

Words appearing in bold, **like this**, are explained in the Glossary.

WHAT IS BODY PIERCING?

Body piercings

Body piercing means just what it sounds like – deliberately making a hole in your body. The hole usually goes through the skin, and is designed to hold a piece of jewellery. For example, millions of people around the world have their earlobes pierced and wear earrings through the holes. Other common places for piercings include the nose, the bottom lip, the tongue and the skin at the top of the navel. Piercings are usually done somewhere that can easily be seen.

The jewellery people wear in their piercings ranges from small, neat rings to bars, dangling chains and spikes. In some societies, people fit large wooden **plugs**, bones, metal discs or even parts of insects into the holes they have made.

This man, one of the Asmat people of Indonesia, has his septum pierced. The large ornament he is wearing through it is carved into a traditional spiral shape.

A long history

Body piercing has a very modern side. Pop stars like Britney Spears and Madonna show off their pierced navels or noses in their videos. Modern **punks** and **goths** wear piercings as part of their culture. In Europe, Australia and the USA, it is now quite usual for teenagers to have their ears or nose pierced as a birthday present.

But piercing is not new. Long before people invented oil paints or canvases, they could express themselves by marking and adorning their own bodies. There is evidence that ancient Egyptian princesses, Aztec priests, Roman soldiers and **prehistoric** peoples all pierced their bodies as decoration.

Why do it?

People pierce their bodies for different reasons. A piercing can show someone belongs to a group or culture. It can be a **rite of passage**, marking the fact that someone has reached a particular age or stage in their life. Sometimes, getting a piercing is a way to rebel against parents, employers or other people in authority.

Some piercings have more specific meanings to do with **status** or religious rituals. For example, among the Tlingit people of Alaska, until the early 20th century, the number of piercings in your ears showed family wealth. In parts of Papua New Guinea, people pierce their noses because they believe it helps them communicate with the spirits of their **ancestors**. Among the Bedouin people of the Middle East, a husband gives his wife a valuable nose ring when they marry. If they get divorced, she can sell the jewel.

However, the biggest reason of all for piercing your body is probably beauty. In most cultures in the world, wearing jewellery through holes in your skin is simply considered attractive. Different piercings are considered acceptable in different cultures. In Britain, ear piercing is so mainstream, at least for women, that MPs, teachers and members of the royal family can all have pierced ears without attracting comment. But piercing your **septum** (the skin between your nostrils), which is common in Papua New Guinea, is often seen as quite shocking in countries like Britain, Australia and the USA.

WHAT ABOUT THE PAIN?

Piercing your body is usually quite painful. It can also be dangerous unless it is done very carefully, with clean equipment. However, most people with piercings consider this a small price to pay for the beauty, attention or sense of belonging they gain from their piercing. In fact, in some societies the pain is an important part of the process. If someone has a piercing, it shows they were old enough and brave enough to put up with the pain.

US pop star Christina Aguilera has her nose pierced and wears multiple earrings.

'He promised me earrings, but he only pierced my ears.'
Arabian proverb

'I thought I was gonna faint. It was really bad, but I don't regret it now. I like it.' US singer Britney Spears talking about having her navel pierced

Risky business

Whenever skin is cut or pierced, germs can get in. They can cause infections that make the skin swollen and painful. If a bad infection gets into someone's bloodstream, it can even be life-threatening, so people who do body piercings have to be very careful.

First, the piercer has to make the hole with a clean needle or other tool. Then the hole has to be kept clean and free of germs until the inside of it has healed. When someone has a new piercing, they may have to bathe it in salt water or use **antibacterial** ointment on it to kill germs.

With most piercings, the piercer makes the hole and leaves a **sterilized** ring, bar or other object in it to stop it from healing and closing up. Gradually, new skin grows along the inside of the hole, the soreness stops and the piercing becomes permanent. People with new piercings may be told to twist or rotate the jewellery (with very clean hands) to help with this process. When the piercing has healed completely and is no longer sore, they can remove the original ring – sometimes called a **keeper** – and put other jewellery in.

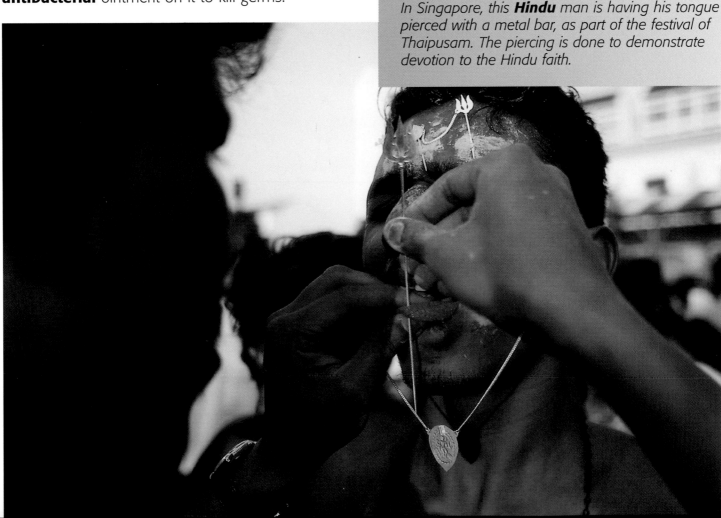

*In Singapore, this **Hindu** man is having his tongue pierced with a metal bar, as part of the festival of Thaipusam. The piercing is done to demonstrate devotion to the Hindu faith.*

FACT

After someone gets their tongue pierced, they have to suck ice cubes to help the swelling go down.

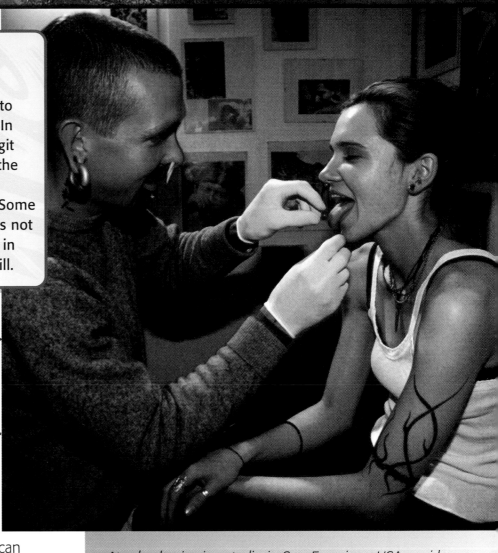

*At a body piercing studio in San Francisco, USA, a girl is having her tongue pierced. The piercer himself has **septum**, ear and lower lip piercings.*

More methods

People all over the world have developed different methods of piercing. The piercing can be done with a metal needle, a sharpened bone or a stone tool, or sometimes a plant thorn. The wound can be kept clean and helped to heal by using the juice or sap from certain wild plants that contain a natural **antiseptic**, such as the tea tree.

Professional piercers in countries such as the USA, Australia, the UK and most of Europe have to follow strict guidelines. They use a brand new, disposable needle for each piercing, and then insert jewellery made of high-quality stainless steel that does not cause **allergic reactions**. They also sterilize all their equipment using a machine called an **autoclave**, which kills germs using very hot steam.

To reduce the pain of a piercing, some piercers put freeze spray on the area to be pierced. It is even possible to have a **local anaesthetic** injection first to make the area completely numb.

REJECTION

The human body has an **immune system** that fights against anything alien inserted into the skin. If a piercing is inserted correctly and kept clean, the body protects itself by healing up the skin around the metal, and the piercing stays in place. But sometimes, especially with navel and eyebrow piercings, the body rejects the metal and pushes it out of the skin.

⚠ Safety

For more advice and information about safety and getting a piercing, see page 31.

ANCIENT PIERCINGS

The earliest piercings

No one knows exactly when the first body piercings took place, but it was certainly thousands of years ago. A 5000-year-old mummy discovered in the Alps in 1991 had pierced ears. The Amazons, a legendary warrior people who may have lived in central Asia around 3000 BC, were said to pierce their ears and noses. An Iranian statue from 5500 years ago has ears that are pierced in several places.

In some ancient societies, the ritual of doing the piercing was the most important part. Among the Inca people, who lived in South America, soldiers used plant thorns or spines from fish to pierce their lips and tongues as a sign of bravery.

Some ancient piercings were a sign of high **status**. In ancient Egypt, for example, you could only have your navel pierced if you were a priest or a member of the royal family. Among the Mayans of Central America, a **labret** piercing showed that you were rich and respectable.

MAGIC PIERCINGS?

Experts have suggested that some very ancient piercings were done as a form of magic, to guard orifices (entrances to the body) against evil spirits. So an earring, for example, would stop evil forces from entering your ear, and a lip ring would prevent them from getting in through your mouth.

This is a statue of Akhenaton, a powerful ancient Egyptian ruler who lived in the 14th century BC. You can see his navel piercing, which was a symbol of his power and royal status.

This carving, from around the 8th century BC, was found in the area that is now Iran. It shows that ear-piercing and large hoop earrings have a long history.

FACT

As well as piercing themselves, ancient humans learned to pierce their domestic animals. Nose-rings have been used to tether horses and oxen for thousands of years.

BIBLE PIERCINGS

Piercing is mentioned several times in the Old Testament of the Bible, an ancient holy book of the Jews and Christians. In the book of Exodus, it describes how a servant would have his ear pierced with an **awl** as a mark of loyalty to his master. Also, in the book of Genesis, Rebekah is given a golden *shanf* – which can mean either an earring or a nose-ring. However, in Leviticus (19:28) it says that people should not pierce themselves. (See page 22.)

Body art clues

Many ancient peoples buried their dead with elaborate ceremonies. As well as the body, they put the person's precious possessions, including jewellery, into the grave. This was so they could take their wealth and favourite possessions with them to the **afterlife**. By looking at these grave goods, we can find out what kind of piercings people had. For example, Scythian tombs dating from about 500 BC, found in present-day Russia, contain elaborate golden earrings. We can also find out about ancient piercings from pictures, such as the art the ancient Egyptians painted inside their tombs and palaces.

SOUTH-EAST ASIA AND AUSTRALIA

Aboriginal art

The Australian Aborigines are the **indigenous** people of Australia, and may have lived there for 40,000 years or more. Their culture includes tongue piercing as part of sacred rituals. These were designed to impress the invisible spirits whom the Aborigines believe in. Because these piercings were temporary and did not involve wearing jewellery, it is very hard for experts to be sure how early they began. However, some experts believe that Aboriginal tongue piercing may well have been the first body piercing in the world.

Australian Aborigines also practise piercing as a **rite of passage**. It is common for young men to have their **septums** pierced to mark their coming-of-age. Some Aborigine women also have pierced septums.

Religious rituals

In South-east Asia, many people take part in temporary ritual piercings as part of religious festivals. **Hindus** in Singapore have their bodies pierced at the festival of Thaipusam, which is held to celebrate the birthday of a Hindu deity called Lord Subramaniam. They have their bodies pierced in order to show their devotion to their faith. Some men have dozens of metal rods or needles inserted into the skin on their chests and legs, while others decorate their faces with fine metal skewers. The insertions are taken out after a few hours. In Malaysia, to celebrate the same festival, people have limes or tiny pots of liquid attached to piercings in their backs. All these rituals are designed to show devotion to Lord Subramaniam and keep him happy.

This man, one of the Walpiri Aboriginal people from the Tanami Desert in Australia, wears a large nose ornament in his septum piercing.

An Orang Ulu woman from Borneo is wearing heavy weights on the ends of her elongated ear-loops.

Ear-stretching

Among some of the peoples of South-east Asia, it is considered particularly beautiful if you gradually stretch a pierced ear into a long loop. Orang Ulu women from Borneo do this by wearing heavily weighted earrings that slowly **elongate** the earlobe. The Kayaw people, who live in Burma and Thailand, achieve a similar effect by inserting increasingly large metal discs or loops into their ear-piercings.

Some piercing enthusiasts in countries like the UK and the USA are now copying this look. They start by using stainless-steel earrings of increasing thicknesses, and eventually make the piercing so big it can hold a hollow tube called an **earlet**, or hang down in a loop.

Tongue piercings are increasingly popular today. They might seem like a modern invention, but in fact, Australian Aboriginies have been piercing their tongues for up to 40,000 years.

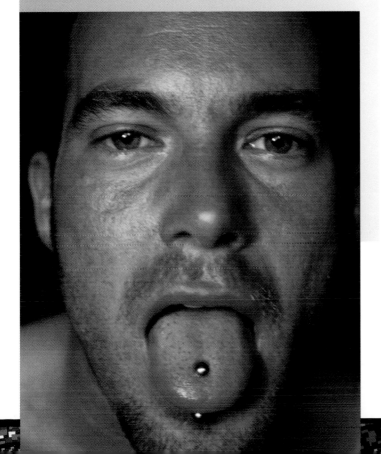

FACT

Statues of the Buddha, the founder of the Buddhist religion, often show him with long, stretched earlobe piercings.

AFRICA

Changing the body

Body modification of all kinds, including piercing, body painting and **tattooing**, has played an important part in many African societies for hundreds or even thousands of years. Today, body piercing is practised less often than it used to be, but there is still a huge range of body piercing styles and jewellery.

When European explorers first arrived in Africa during the 15th century, many of them saw people's pierced noses and lips as a sign of savagery. The Africans thought the opposite; to them, making permanent changes to the body was a way of showing you were civilized, and different from animals.

Lip plugs

A lip **plug** is a disc or plate, usually made of wood or clay, that fits into an enlarged piercing in the lip. Lip plugs range from the size of a coin to the size of a dinner plate.

Among the Surma of Ethiopia, young women start to enlarge their lower lip before getting married. They insert bigger and bigger plugs into the lip to stretch it. After only about six months, the lip is big enough to hold a plug as big as a CD. Women with lip plugs wear them at all times in public, only removing them to sleep and eat in private. When a woman gets married, the size of her lip plate is seen as a measure of her beauty. It decides her 'bride-price' – the fee her new husband must pay to marry her.

The Kichepo people of Sudan have a similar tradition, but it is slowly dying out. Only a few women still wear huge lip plugs. Nowadays, most Kichepo girls wear a small lip piercing to **symbolize** their membership of the group.

For many African peoples, lip plugs give a person extra **status** in their society. The bigger the plug, the higher the status.

FACT

Turkana people from East Africa wear large leaf-shaped aluminium jewels in their noses to announce that their daughter has got engaged.

This young Surma woman is wearing a large round wooden lip plug in her lower lip. Plugs can be round or square. In this photo, you can also see the girl's enlarged ear piercing. As well as lip plugs, Surma women often wear heavy, decorated earlobe plugs made out of clay.

This Masai woman from Kenya is wearing very large beaded earrings in her multiple, stretched piercings.

Ear adornments

Ear piercings can be in any part of the ear. Instead of a ring, Kirdi people from Cameroon wear metal spikes, like small daggers, through the tops of their ears. The Mangbetu, from the Democratic Republic of Congo, make a hole through the back of the ear and wear a rod that reaches through and rests against the back of the head.

Masai piercings

The Masai, a famous group from Kenya and Tanzania, often pierce their ears in several places. For special occasions, they wear elaborate beaded jewellery and chains that link the separate holes together, or connect the ear to other parts of their head.

Fulani piercings

Wealthy Fulani women from Mali wear enormous gold earrings in order to show off their riches. The earrings are very heavy, so to stop the earlobes from stretching too much, the women sometimes wear a strap over their heads to hold the earrings up. Women often pass their earrings down to their daughters or nieces, so that their wealth stays with the women of their own family.

CROSSING THE GLOBE

In many parts of the world today, people have a row of holes pierced in each earlobe, like the Masai. It is also fashionable to pierce other parts of the ear, such as the **tragus** or the rook (the top of the ear). A piercing that connects several parts of the ear with one piece of jewellery is known as an 'ear project'.

THE ARCTIC

Arctic peoples

The Arctic is the area around the North Pole. It is home to groups such as the Inuit, Aleut, Tlingit and Lapps. Until recently, wood and metal were hard to obtain in the icy Arctic, so these peoples developed the use of use animal bones for their body-piercing tools and jewellery.

Potlatch piercings

For the Tlingit people from Alaska, body piercing was traditionally about showing off your wealth. It was used in this way until the early 20th century. If a Tlingit man wanted to impress his neighbours, he would throw a party called a **potlatch** to show how rich he was. At the potlach, the local ear-piercer was paid vast sums to pierce the ears of the host's children and grandchildren.

After several potlatches, the children of the wealthiest families would have rows of piercings in their ears. Throughout their lives, these marks would act as a **symbol** of their high standing in society.

Nose piercings were popular with the Tlingit, for both men and women, as a mark of **status**. Today, many of the old Tlingit traditions have died out, but some Tlingit preserve their culture and wear traditional costumes for celebrations and special occasions.

FACT

Some Inuit lip piercings were so big, the plugs had to be taken out for eating and speaking.

*This Tlingit woman was photographed in 1906, before Tlingit piercing traditions died out. She is wearing face paint and a **septum** ring as part of a potlatch dancing costume.*

The Inuit

The Inuit live mainly in Northern Canada and Greenland. Until the end of the 19th century, they pierced their lips and cheeks as **rites of passage**. Wearing lip **plugs** was a sign that a person had reached adulthood, and like many other peoples, the Inuit often stretched their piercings to hold bigger and bigger plugs. Inuit women usually had a single **labret** piercing under the lower lip, while men wore two piercings, in the upper lips or on the sides of the face.

Inuit piercings were partly done to guard against evil spirits entering the mouth, but they had another purpose, too. When the men went hunting, they would wear rods through the piercings in their cheeks to imitate a walrus's whiskers. They believed that this gave them a better chance of catching a walrus.

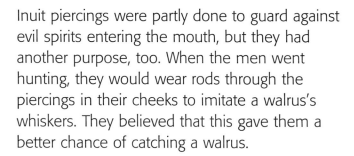

These labret jewels are thought to have belonged to a wealthy Inuit man from northwest Alaska. They would have been worn through piercings on either side of the lower lip.

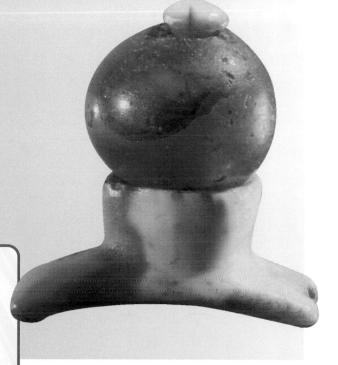

BONE AND STONE

As there was a shortage of wood in the Arctic, and it was hard to get metal out of the frozen ground, Alaskan peoples used mainly stone or bone to make their jewellery. The Tlingit made earrings out of sharks' teeth, while 19th-century Inuit lip plugs could be carved from walrus bone or seashells, or from minerals such as marble, jade or granite. To make the holes, the Inuit used tiny, very sharp blades made from slate.

CHEEK PIERCING TODAY

Cheek piercings are rare in Europe, Australia and the USA, but they are starting to be revived. Piercers consider them very hard to do because the cheek contains many nerves and blood vessels which must be carefully avoided. Some cheek piercings go right through the cheek, while others run just under the skin. They are known as **surface-to-surface** piercings.

INDIA

Garlanded in gold

In Indian society, many people wear a lot of gold jewellery, especially for special occasions like weddings. Pierced noses and multiple ear piercings make space for as many jewels as possible. India is one of the world's biggest countries and many different peoples live there, with different religions and ways of life, and different piercing styles and customs.

Nose piercing

Nose piercing – in the side of the nose, rather than through the **septum** – is a typical Indian adornment. It is thought to have originated in the Middle East around 4000 years ago, and made its way from there to India roughly 500 years ago. In the 16th and 17th centuries it was fashionable for royalty and aristocracy to pierce their noses, and today millions of Indian women wear a jewel in their nose. A nose stud is called a *phul*, while a ring is known as a *nath*.

NOSE JEWELS

Here are some names for different types of nose jewellery worn in India:

- *nath*: a nose ring. One side may be decorated with precious stones or pearls
- *bulak*: a dangling chain, worn through a nose piercing or attached to a nath
- *latkan*: a set of pendants attached to a nath
- *laung*: a small metal nose stud, sometimes decorated with a pearl or a piece of precious stone
- *phuli*: a small nose ring with an oval jewel hanging from it

Most Indian women have their nose pierced on the left-hand side. Traditionally, this was thought to make childbirth easier. In some areas, people pierced their left nostril if they wanted their children to be boys, and their right nostril if they wanted to have girls.

Many people from an Indian background now live in Europe, the USA, Africa and other parts of the world, but still wear a traditional nose piercing. This bride, in Southall in the UK, is wearing a nose stud for her Sikh wedding.

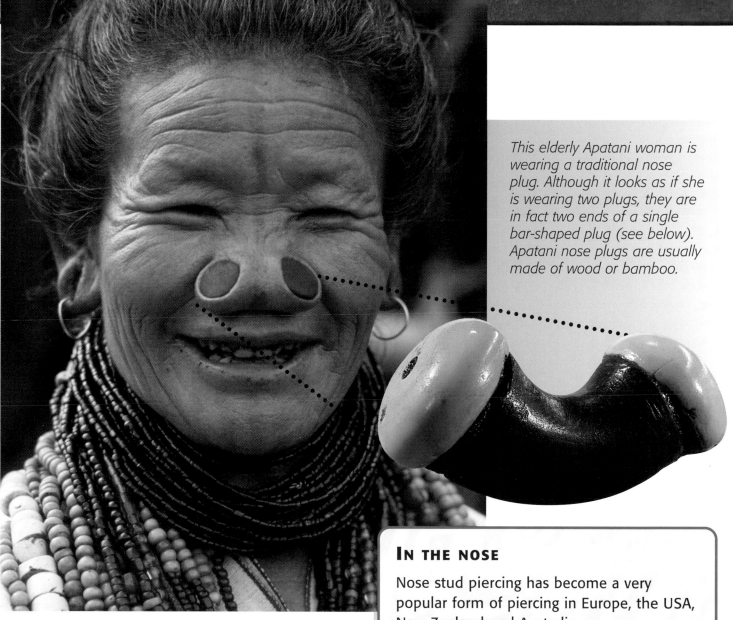

This elderly Apatani woman is wearing a traditional nose plug. Although it looks as if she is wearing two plugs, they are in fact two ends of a single bar-shaped plug (see below). Apatani nose plugs are usually made of wood or bamboo.

Nose plugs

In Arunachal Pradesh, in the mountainous north-east of India, live the Apatani people, who have developed an unusual kind of piercing. Apatani women wear a thick, curved **plug** through the centre of the nose, with its ends filling two enlarged nose piercings.

Like many piercing practices around the world, this type of piercing is now dying out, and only older women can be seen wearing the plug. According to local legend, this piercing was done because the Apatani believed the female members of their group were so beautiful they might be kidnapped by neighbouring tribes. The nose plug was designed to put them off.

IN THE NOSE

Nose stud piercing has become a very popular form of piercing in Europe, the USA, New Zealand and Australia.

A nose stud cannot stick straight through the side of your nose, because it would poke the sensitive inside of your nose and make it sore. Instead, the jewel has a flat surface on the inside, or is curved round so that it lies flat against the inside of your nose.

Piercing and holy men

A **sadhu** is an Indian holy man. *Sadhus* devote their lives to religion and meditation. Some can achieve a trance-like state of mind in which they feel no pain. At **Hindu** religious festivals in India, you can sometimes see *sadhus* piercing their tongues and cheeks to demonstrate this. They believe that performing these ascetic (self-sacrificing) rituals brings them closer to their gods.

EUROPE

Body art ban

Christianity spread through Europe between AD 100 and AD 900. Because part of the Bible contains a ban on marking and piercing the body, Christian leaders told some European peoples, such as the **Celts** and the **Picts**, to stop **tattooing**, painting and piercing themselves. Body art was seen as a sign of belonging to old, **pagan** religions, so for a long time it was frowned upon. However, it was to return.

In the late 15th and early 16th centuries, Spanish and Portuguese explorers travelled to the Americas, where they encountered groups of peoples such as the Aztecs, with their pierced lips and gold and jade jewellery. In the 17th and 18th centuries, the British and Dutch went to Australia and the Pacific Islands, and sailors copied some of the styles they found there, returning home with tattoos and pierced ears.

Traditions from abroad

From **medieval** times onwards, Europeans began exploring the rest of the world and were re-introduced to body piercing through the art of the peoples they met.

MULTICULTURAL PIERCINGS

From the 15th to the 19th centuries, European countries took over and controlled many parts of the world. They were influenced by the people who lived in the countries they ruled, and eventually a lot of those people – Indians, Arabians, Africans, Indonesians and so on – went to settle in Europe. Countries like Britain, France and Holland are now much more **multicultural** than before, and now activities such as nose piercing are widely practised there.

This 17th-century painting of Anne Boleyn, the second wife of Henry VIII and Queen of England from 1533–1536, shows her wearing an elaborate earring.

By the 16th century, piercing the ears, and sometimes other body parts, was fashionable all over Europe, even in high society. Even the 19th-century Victorians, who are often seen today as very straight-laced, made body piercing a part of their culture. But as time wore on, it became less popular. Women could pierce their ears, but other piercings became uncommon.

Hippies and punks

Interest in body piercing started to pick up again in the 1960s, a time of great change and experimentation in Europe. Young Europeans travelled to India and the Far East to find out about different religions and lifestyles. They came back sporting types of body art which were unusual in Europe at the time, such as nose piercings.

In the 1970s, the rebellious **punk** movement took off. It used **body modification** as a way of trying to rebel against rules and upset those in authority. Punks had multiple piercings in their noses, cheeks or eyebrows. They wore chains and safety pins through their skin in an attempt to look frightening and shocking.

EYEBROW PIERCING

Eyebrow piercing is one piercing that seems to have been invented quite recently, and today it is very popular. An eyebrow piercing normally contains a **barbell** or steel ring.

The eyebrow is usually pierced at the outer end. Piercers have to be careful to avoid the centre of the eyebrow because it contains an important nerve that controls the eyelid. If this nerve is damaged, it can make the eyelid droop.

EARS AROUND THE WORLD

Popular piercing

Ear piercing is the most popular piercing around the world. Even people who disapprove of navel, lip, tongue and eyebrow piercing may themselves have pierced ears. From India to Italy, Borneo to Brazil, cultures in every part of the world have independently discovered and developed ear piercing. Even some of the ancient, mysterious statues on Easter Island appear to have pierced ears. Why is ear piercing so popular? The earlobe is soft and easy to pierce, and heals well. It has very few nerve endings, so it is not too painful. Best of all, earlobes are almost always on display, so they make a great place to show off your jewels.

Playwrights and sailors

In Europe today, it is more unusual for men to have pierced ears, but this was not always the case. In the 16th century, wealthy men, such as the explorer Walter Raleigh and the playwright William Shakespeare, often had an ear pierced. For centuries, sailors and fishermen wore gold earrings – partly so that if they died and were washed up on a foreign shore, the gold in the earring could be used to pay for a decent funeral. The Roman leader Julius Caesar set a trend by wearing earrings in both ears, encouraging other wealthy citizens to copy him.

Ear piercing practices

Professional body piercers say that the only safe way to have your ear pierced is with a **sterile** needle. However, millions of people still have their ears pierced in jeweller's shops or department stores with a piercing gun. This is a specially built machine that fires a stud earring through your ear at high speed. Piercing guns, if not cleaned properly, can be less hygenic than a sterile needle.

Some Amazon **rainforest** peoples pierce their ears with a sharpened stick. Other South American groups use a plant thorn or a sharp animal bone. Some 19th-century American pioneers used a hot needle, with a potato held behind the ear for the needle to stick into.

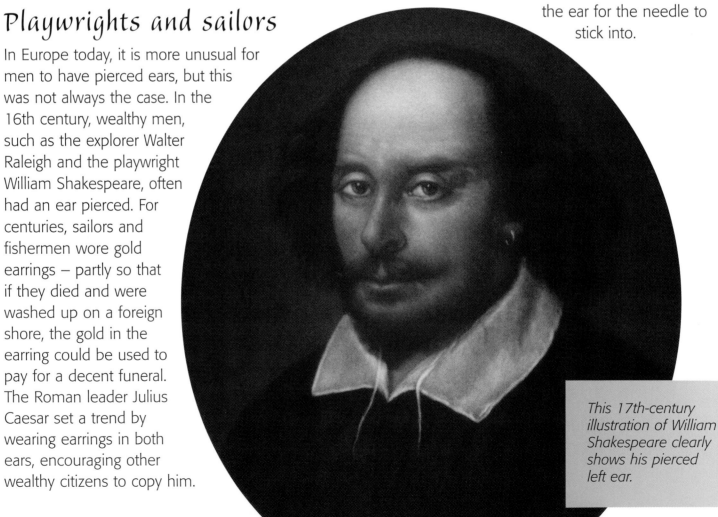

This 17th-century illustration of William Shakespeare clearly shows his pierced left ear.

FACT

In ancient Assyria, the type of earring a man wore showed his rank in society.

Ear meanings

Like many other piercings, ear piercings can have a **symbolic** value. In **medieval** Britain a pierced ear was thought to protect your health. The Suya people from West Africa pierce their children's ears because it is said to help them to listen. As they get older, the children wear larger ear **plugs**, which are thought to make them good at learning. In Naga villages in India, fathers will pierce the ears of their children soon after birth to welcome them into the family.

EARS AND EYESIGHT

Pictures of pirates often show them with gold earrings. Pirates did wear earrings – probably partly to show off the stolen gold they had amassed. But it was also because seafarers used to believe that piercing your ears led to improved eyesight (useful for a life at sea). For a long time this was thought to be just a myth, but there may actually be some truth in it. The part of the earlobe where earrings are positioned has an **acupuncture** point that relates to eyesight, and stimulating that point may make your eyes work better.

Here the singer and film star Jennifer Lopez wears large valuable earrings to an Oscar ceremony. Like people throughout history, she is using her ear piercings to display expensive jewellery, showing off her wealth and **status**.

THE REVIVAL OF PIERCING

Body art boom

Along with other forms of body art like **tattooing**, piercing is now more popular than ever across the world. Almost every big city has at least one professional piercing studio where people can have their piercings done in a safe, clean environment. Jewellery shops stock not just earrings, but belly button rings, nose jewels and **barbells** too.

Although piercing enthusiasts sometimes invent new piercings, most styles are influenced by practices from around the world. Even as these traditions die out in their original homes, they influence the people of places like the USA, Europe and Japan.

Being different

Many people with piercings say they feel that modern society tries to force-feed them idealized images of beauty through adverts, magazines and TV shows. Body piercing is a way to react against these pressures. It lets people experiment with different concepts of beauty – which are often much older than those portrayed in today's media.

However, some types of body piercing are now so normal that they have become part of the mainstream. Navel piercing, for example, is common among female pop stars and models, and is also worn by millions of ordinary women and girls as well as some men.

> POPULAR PIERCINGS
>
> Here are some of today's most popular piercings, along with the time each one takes to heal:
> - earlobe   4–8 weeks
> - **tragus**   4 months to 1 year
> - eyebrow   6–8 weeks
> - nostril   2–4 months
> - **septum**   6–8 months
> - tongue   4–6 weeks
> - lip   2–3 months
> - navel   4 months to 1 year

*This piercing devotee has dozens of eyebrow, septum, nose, lip and ear piercings, and **surface-to-surface** piercings in his cheeks and forehead.*

In 1997, a 15-year-old British girl survived being hit by lightning when her metal navel ring diverted the deadly electrical charge away from her chest.

People who are really keen on piercing have their own clubs and magazines where they can discuss their hobby. They meet up at piercing conventions where they can compare their body art and learn new styles. Among devoted piercers, body piercing and other kinds of body art are known as **body modification** or Bod-Mod.

During a concert, the pop star Britney Spears wears an outfit that reveals her navel jewellery.

TONGUE TROUBLE

As well as reaching back many centuries, tongue piercing is very popular today. When it is first pierced, the tongue swells up so much that piercers have to start with an extra-long bar, and then change it to a shorter one when the swelling goes down. The wound often gets infected with bacteria, and even if it heals successfully, the metal bar can sometimes chip your teeth! Tongue piercing has been made popular by several famous wearers, such as Janet Jackson, former Spice Girl Mel B and Zara Phillips, a young member of the British royal family (shown here in 1998). It is still seen as quite rebellious, yet it is also easy to keep hidden.

New Directions

New and old

As piercing becomes more common, enthusiasts are searching for more exciting and unusual piercings. Many of the new ideas they come up with are influenced by piercing styles from around the world. They include piercing the sides of the cheeks, as the Inuit used to, and wearing long spikes, rods or tusk-shaped jewels through the **septum**, like the peoples of Papua New Guinea. Some people have many shallow **surface-to-surface** piercings done all over their backs, similar to the ceremonial piercings worn for the Thaipusam festival in South-east Asia. Also like the Aztecs, Kayaw, Kayapo and many other peoples from around the world, some piercing fans have started to stretch the holes in their ears, noses or lips to hold large **plugs**.

Rituals and rites

For groups like the Surma of Africa, the Inuit and the Kayapo, a piercing was traditionally a **rite of passage**, marking the fact that a person had reached a certain age or position in society. In countries like the USA and Australia, parents often allow their children to have a piercing only when they reach a certain age. So for many young people, ear, tongue or navel piercings are also a rite of passage, marking a particular birthday, such as sixteen, when they are considered old enough to make their own decisions. Many people now see the piercing itself as not just a painful moment to endure, but as a special occasion, marking a change in a person's life.

UNDER THE SKIN

To change their appearance, some people have steel rods, balls or studs buried right under their skin and sewn in. Or they have permanent base studs fixed into the skin – on the scalp, for example – which can have additional parts, such as metal spikes, screwed into them as the wearer chooses.

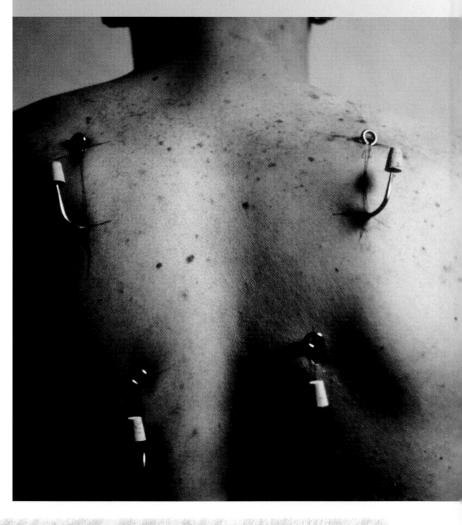

Piercings are getting more outrageous all the time. This man has had fish hooks inserted all over his back.

'I got my first two lobe piercings (one in each ear) when I was much younger but each of the last four was to mark closures, turning points or triumphs in my life.' A piercing fan, aged 22, from the USA

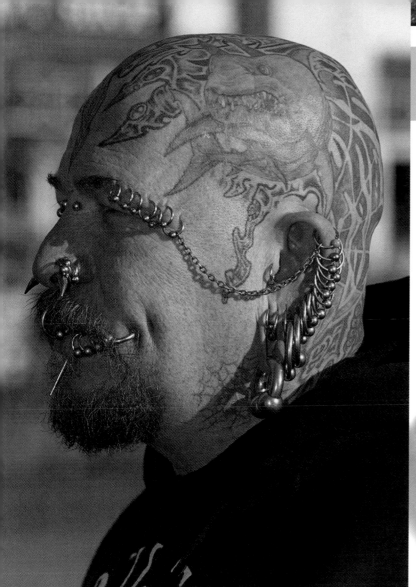

POCKETING

Piercing enthusiasts have invented a new type of piercing called pocketing. Instead of making a tunnel through your flesh, pocketing simply makes a shallow hole, or pocket, in your skin. The pockets are usually made in pairs. When the piercing heals, you can wear metal bands on your skin. The ends of the bands fit into the pockets, so it looks as if your skin has been stapled.

Wilder and weirder

Piercers today are inventing many brand-new body piercings. Some people now have **barbells** or rings inserted into the webbing between fingers or toes, across the bridge of the nose, through the chin, or even through the uvula, the small lump of flesh that hangs down at the back of the throat. Surface-to-surface piercings can be done almost anywhere – on the wrists, arms, shoulders, neck, stomach, legs, feet and hands. One type of surface piercing looks just like a normal finger ring, but instead of surrounding the finger, the ring goes right through it.

This pierced Barbie doll, designed in 2000 by the clothes designer Jean-Paul Gaultier, shows how much piercing has become a part of youth culture today.

FURTHER INFORMATION

Safety tips

! Think carefully before getting a body piercing. It can be expensive and will probably leave a permanent mark, so make sure you know what you want and are 100 per cent sure before you go ahead.

! If you are under eighteen, most piercing studios will require you to have your parents' permission. It is even better if you can take a parent with you when you have your piercing done.

! Avoid extreme or unusual piercings, as they are most likely to go wrong or be hard to look after. Ears and navels are the most popular and safest places for piercings.

! The best way to have your navel pierced is to lie down on a bed or table, so it will not matter if you feel faint.

! Always go to a professional piercing studio that uses sterile equipment and follows safety guidelines. Ask to see the work area before you make any decisions. If the staff do not want to talk about safety and cleanliness, go somewhere else.

! After getting a piercing done, follow the piercer's cleaning and care instructions exactly.

! Never touch a piercing with dirty hands.

! Wear clean clothing and change bedding every week while piercings are healing.

! Avoid make-up, powders, perfumes and hairsprays in the piercing area during healing.

! Make sure any jewellery in mouth piercings is tightly in place, so you do not swallow it or damage your teeth.

Books

The Body Decorated, Victoria Ebin (Thames and Hudson, 1979)

The Decorated Body, Robert Brain (Hutchison, 1979)

Decorated Skin, Karl Groning (Thames and Hudson, 1997)

Tattooing and Body Piercing: Understanding the Risks, Kathleen Winkler (Enslow, 2002)

Websites

http://www.museum.upenn.edu/new/ exhibits/online_exhibits/body_modification/ bodmodintro.shtml
University of Pennsylvania Museum of Archaeology and Anthropology's 'Bodies of Cultures' online exhibition

http://www.tattoosdownunder.com.au/ museum.html
Body Art at the Australian Museum, Sydney

http://www.vh.org/pediatric/patient/ dermatology/tattoo
University of Iowa's Virtual Hospital: Tattooing and Body Piercing: Decision Making for Teens

Places to visit

Costume museums may have exhibits relating to body piercing from time to time. So will other regional museums – check your local newspaper for listings, or look in the national listings pages of daily newspapers, which often have this information on Saturdays.

GLOSSARY

acupuncture   Chinese medical treatment that works by inserting needles into the skin at certain points to stimulate parts of the body to heal

afterlife   another life or spiritual existence which some people believe we live after death

allergic reaction   rash, swelling or sneezing caused by the body's reaction to a normally harmless substance

Amerindian   people descended from those who lived in South America before Europeans arrived there

ancestor   family member who lived a long time ago

antibacterial   containing chemicals that kill bacteria

antiseptic   substance that prevents germs from multiplying

archipelago   group of islands

ascetic   leading a life of self-denial or suffering, usually for religious reasons

autoclave   machine used for sterilizing piercing equipment and jewellery

awl   sharp pointed tool

barbell   metal bar with a ball at each end, often worn in body piercings

body modification   (or Bod-Mod) name body art enthusiasts give to body piercing, tattooing and other kinds of permanent body art

Buddhist   a member of the Buddhist religion, which follows the teachings of a prophet called the Buddha

Celts   peoples who were originally from the north-western fringes of Europe, especially Wales, Ireland and Scotland

ear spool   kind of ear plug

earlet   hollow ring designed to fit inside a stretched ear piercing

elongate   to stretch and make longer

goth   used to describe a style of fashion involving dark-coloured clothes and heavy make-up

Hinduism   religion popular in India and South-east Asia

immune system   organs and cells that fight germs and foreign objects that enter the body

indigenous   belonging to a place. For example, the Inuit people are indigenous to Arctic regions of North America.

keeper   ring or stud used to keep a piercing open when it has just been done, or when you are not wearing more elaborate jewellery

labret   piercing in the upper or lower lip

local anaesthetic   injection or spray that dulls pain in a particular area of your body

medieval   time period stretching from approximately AD 500 to 1500

multicultural   containing many different cultures

Native American   first peoples of North America. There are still many Native Americans living in Canada and the USA.

pagan   this can mean a type of religion that has many gods, or a non-Christian religion. It can also be used to mean having no religion at all.

perception   ability to experience things using your senses

Picts   ancient people who lived in the area that is now Scotland up until about AD 900

plug   large cylinder or plate designed to be worn in a stretched piercing. Lip plugs, nose plugs and ear plugs are all types of plugs.

potlatch   traditional Native American feast at which people show off their wealth

prehistoric   time up to about 10,000 years ago, before history started to be written down

punk   originally meaning a lazy or worthless young person, this word is now mainly used to describe a rebellious music and fashion movement that began in Europe in the 1960s

rainforest   type of thick, hot, rainy forest found in parts of the world around the equator, such as Central Africa, South-east Asia and Central and South America

rite of passage   ceremony held to celebrate reaching a certain age or stage of life

sadhu   holy man who lives a life of meditation or self-deprivation

septum   skin between your nostrils

status   standing or reputation in society

sterile/sterilize   completely clean and free from harmful germs. If you sterilize something, you make it sterile.

surface-to-surface   type of shallow piercing that runs just under the skin

symbol/symbolize   something that stands for, or symbolizes, an idea

tattoo   permanent mark made on the body by inserting ink under the skin with a needle

tragus   the flap of skin just in front of the ear hole

INDEX